open book

—

Valerie Coulton

Apogee Press
Berkeley · California
2011

Many thanks to the editors of *Front Porch, kadar koli,* and *e-poema,* in which some of these pieces first appeared.

With deepest gratitude to Carmina for friendship and inspiration, to Quim for being such a great scalphunter, and to Iñigo for light and walls. Thanks to Kate Simer and Emilie Delcourt for all the readings at Collage, and to Alena Widows and Harriet Sandilands for support and inspiration. With thanks to Mairi Alexopoulou, Vassilis Manoussakis, Phoebe Giannisi, Socrates Kabouropoulos and Katerina Illiopoulou for friendship, inspiration, and for translating some of these poems into Greek. And with thanks to Carmen Cadierna, Pilar Sturla, Mabel Sorraco, Elena Martí and my students and colleagues at InfoJobs, for making me feel at home in Barcelona.

Thank you, Edward, *for this life.*

Cover painting: *La lunette d'approche (The Telescope),* by Rene Magritte ©2011 C. Herscovici, London / Artists Rights Society (ARS), New York The Menil Collection, Houston. Photographer: Hickey-Robertson, Houston

Book cover and interior design by Philip Krayna at NKD www.nkdesigngroup.com

ISBN 978-0-9787667-8-8. Library of Congress Catalog Card Number 2011923022.

Published by Apogee Press, 2308 Sixth Street, Berkeley CA, 94710. www.apogeepress.com

Table of Contents

Somos tiempo, tiempo y agua.
Somos tiempo, agua y deseo.
Nubes que hablan,
túneles en la niebla.

—Íñigo Amézola

libro borrado

for my parents, and for Carmina

Plaça del Diamant

There are many places I never go and it would be pointless to name them, perhaps even wrong to do so. These are sentences I formed earlier, before the loud celebration began somewhere nearby. To name a place is to imply some familiarity with it, a subjective relation. This neighborhood is full of streets and squares which once had other names. Soon their names will change again, like this wind which keeps shifting directions. Who am I to say? The man across the way has stopped yelling. Clouds hover. A woman yells, she snarls. This is what we call the simple present, used to describe permanent or habitual states and actions. Also used for effect in writing, especially when suspense is desirable. It is already darker earlier now. I'm forgetting what I wanted to write. Something to do with nouns and emotional states, the absurdity (immorality?) of supposing that a noun such as *happiness* means anything at all, much less something communicable in language, something specific. The present continuous has come in, keeps coming in. People are opening doors and walking into squares. Televisions are flickering. The bell tower with its zodiac design is about to strike.

La Peluquería

Pelo, a word for hair, close to the word for skin, *piel*. *Piel* can also be leather, an equals sign unsurprising in a country where the hams still have their hooves. They hang from the ceiling on hooks, with small umbrella-shaped cups stuck into them to catch the oil. If you look closely at your arm, you see the grain of the skin. When I was born, I had a great deal of hair. Even now, when the tufts of cut hair that fall all around me are half gray, the hairdresser says *"tu tienes mucho pelo."* We've passed midsummer. The square is full of women and girls, eating ice cream, parading and singing, holding hands, holding a dog's leash. When you are young, your hair may be long or cut in the style they used to call "pageboy." Your mother has most of the say in this decision; she's the one who'll wash your hair and fasten your plastic barrettes, or gather it into a ponytail. When my mother was a little girl, she wanted curls like Shirley Temple. I wanted to write something about my mother's lifelong dissatisfaction with her hair, but then the jackhammer started, the gypsies came to beg and stayed too long, dropping trash at my feet as they left to try the next café. I'm a foreigner here, an American. I look for signs of being treated differently, even by the two gypsy women who canvass the neighborhood day after day. The three old women have finished their ice cream. Girls in halter tops and bright skirts cross and re-cross the square. I might be described here if someone else were writing this—a woman at a table in the corner, an *extranjera*, not quite invisible, waiting to be seen.

Los Guantes

The box in the car was supposed to be for gloves, but was full
of maps instead. Maps, and odd bits of paper, and old
peppermints from restaurants. I would fly the car, in my
Amelia Earhart days, from its place in the driveway up and out
over the ocean. You could die in the ocean, or disappear. Under
its net of light another world began.

El Madrugador

The Count of Monte Cristo's incarceration comes to pass primarily through a single letter, which names him as part of a conspiracy to overthrow Louis XVIII and restore Napoleon to power. After many years imprisoned, the young man befriends a fellow prisoner, Abbé Faria, who educates him and bequeaths him the fortune which provides the instrument of his revenge. Faria also reveals the secret of the letter: the writer has written it with his left hand. I had difficulty learning to write. I held my pencil at an odd angle and I was confounded by the letter A, which seemed to me to be upside down compared with my own letter V, the first one I learned to make. My left-handed father arched his wrist around the page and swept across it with a graceful, steady script. My mother's hand seemed was rounded and brisk by comparison. At a certain age I decided to differentiate my writing from theirs, to make my letters architectural and modern, to render my signature a distinctive, indecipherable scribble. My mother objected. My father seemed pleased. It's difficult, now, to stop reading *The Count of Monte Cristo*. The weight and thickness of the book give me a comforting sense of continuation and longevity. In addition, it seems that the pleasure Dumas took in writing the book is constantly present. I would read late into the night, sometimes until dawn, often one of the books left over from my parents' English teaching days. The world of books seemed inexhaustible then, even though I realize now that our library was quite small. I would fall asleep at last, replete with the populous solitude of reading. Meanwhile, in another part of the house, my father would be waking in the chalky, promising light.

El Tiempo

Time and weather—we went/we were—some misunderstandings can't be explained by the change of language. Was I distracted, or did I have ulterior motives? One of my students tried to explain an emotional (psychological?) state with a word that seemed to mean something like "muddy water," but this is probably a misunderstanding too—another failure to communicate. Clouds arrived and thickened the air. I was thinking of my father, but how much was this really a factor? Wants and half-wants; our task is explaining the meaning of words to each other. Then we practice using them together. I am often asked questions I can't answer. The clouds move diagonally overhead, towards the sea where we might or might not have lunch, depending on the weather. My thoughts stray in the same direction. But the sea is already full of glass and plastic and the jellyfish we call *medusas*. If you swim among them, they will break into pieces and stick to you. A woman's cigarette smoke blows my way. The square is full of people and shadow. My father used to take me to the drugstore for an ice cream cone. The scoop had an odd shape, producing a short cylinder; my father always ordered Rocky Road. I don't see what he has to do with this hour and these clouds. I don't recall him explaining the definition of a word, except perhaps the word *gentilesse*, which he said came from Chaucer. We were sitting by the water, protected from the wind by a little green hill. Soon we would pack up the remains of our picnic and go our separate ways.

Hostia

My parents were careful not to swear in my presence. I later learned that the words they reserved for this purpose were extremely mild and rather old-fashioned. For them, the intensity of expression mattered more than the words themselves: *it's the way you say it*. My mother would mutter and hiss, as though her rage were forced through a very small opening. My father would swear only when pushed to unaccustomed anger, and then his language retained the wholesome roughness of a freshly sawn 2x4. Mistakes, omissions, accidents, near misses, little sins—these went unremarked, unembellished by the embroidery of cursing. Driving to the shore the other day, a rock flew into the windshield and disappeared, but the sound of the word remained, light and crisp in the air.

El Cine

To speak with pleasure despite difficulties. He goes to the patio to write, to undertake a serious change of life. Immediately, he is interrupted by music, by children. We were sitting in this same square talking about the symbol of a young girl. Certainly she appears in the movie to signify possibility. The shadows are sharp, the light Mediterranean. She will appear again at the end of the film, on the same shore but divided from him by water, sound: a screen that makes communication impossible. Their efforts, at the edge of despair, resemble joy.

Retrato de Carmina con Manitas

I was a bit lost, as usual in those days, walking south along the outside wall of the park looking for a way in. It was one of those holidays I didn't truly understand. I'd passed through the station into the milk-lit neighborhood—the young man I'd thought suspicious finally stopped at a corner and let himself into a shop in order to open it, to push the ice cream freezer out near the street, to take the money from the safe and put it into the cash register. I'd asked another where to find the park, even though I'd been there before. My difficulty in speaking Spanish had erased the route Carmina had led me along. His syllables were thick and vague; I hurried, sweating a little now. The first gate was locked and I imagined the park closed, and her waiting hidden somewhere, on another street probably, wondering. At last I came to an opening. She could see me from her table near the back as I scuffed along. Her hands with their rings were quiet in her lap, and beside her in a chair were two enormous dictionaries: the whole language, which she had somehow carried.

Setas

A change of address. Meaning the previous *you* is not the current *you*. The you who makes the coffee and administers spoonfuls of extra Sunday sleep. You who spoke of mushrooms as magical, mysterious in their nocturnal appearance in the forest. The word *forest* plush with childhood fur and the glitter of spider webs. Here the prized mushrooms are sturdy little tables dappled with green. Are they similar to the ones you hunted with your grandmother? Mushrooms and the words for mushrooms, the earth that clings to each. Were you the one who taught me speech and ink? I can't remember now.

La Vergüenza

One book will be the last book. Tolstoy used this metaphor in *Anna Karenina:* "And the candle by which she had been reading that book that is filled with anxiety, deceit, sorrow and evil flared up with a brighter flame than ever before, lighted up everything for her that had previously been in darkness, flickered, dimmed, and went out forever." But we were speaking of the real act of reading. What will the last book be? If I'd been struck by the bus yesterday, the one that careened into the crosswalk almost against the driver's will, if his face was any indication, the last book would have been *The Invention of Solitude,* in my bag at the time. A weekend of autumn in midsummer. I was walking to the beach to eat paella with some people from work. I knew I'd be the first one to arrive, and I worried that the turnout would be disappointing, since the whole thing had been my idea to begin with. The beach was ugly and urban; a group of shirtless men occupied the nearest restaurant terrace. Music blared across the sand. I have tried to write a few novels, and I must admit I've never been able to finish any of them. My resistance consists of... Well, it would be easy to say a delicacy of shame, an embarrassment, the same impulse that makes me look away from the Englishmen with their blue tattoos and pale skin. But they are not ashamed. My students say this is a culture in which shame has value: it tempers one's behavior. Allegedly the fear of ridicule, of appearing ridiculous, still keeps one in check here, and makes foreigners stand out. A long time ago, looking through old souvenirs together, I found a note my grandmother had written to my mother in anticipation of a Thanksgiving visit to her sorority sister's home in Chicago. Apparently the family was quite wealthy, and the note was full of practical advice, conveyed in a rather urgent tone, about what to pack and how to prepare for the visit. My grandmother, who had never been to college, and whose prior education is unknown to me, had written "be sure" as one word. This word, full of concern and written in her distinctive hand on a company memo pad, was repeated many times.

El Espejo

The perfect man has no face. Behind every story, there is another story. Books multiply and refract. When the wanderer, believed long dead, returns, only one person recognizes him. He has disguised himself artfully but failed to erase all traces of that which was once loved: a tone of voice, a scar, the body's signature by which the soul is written. *You who have grown old in so many mirrors,* naked under your disguise.

Libro Borrado

It would seem that the use of Spanish titles should be abandoned—after all they will soon be erased. Someone has written the word *pencil*, which reminds me of my student's blue Staedtler mechanical, left behind after a particularly enjoyable class in which we made plans to visit the Maritime Museum. Of course we'll never go now. The pencil was translucent and had its own eraser, which my student never used. He preferred a white oval, partly consumed, to efface his misspellings. After he had gone, I used the pencil myself for awhile, to update the files of other students. The lead was very hard and the eraser inadequate. I considered sliding the pencil into my bag. There's another word here somewhere, the word *wish*. The Spanish word for this isn't quite satisfactory—it has its feet too firmly on the ground. *Wish* is for fountains and candles, a word with an old-fashioned kite string rippling out from it. It seems to me we made kites once, but they wouldn't really fly, they were just something to take home to our parents. Someone has written *the subject of all poems is the clock*. Someone else wrote about a unique anxiety: the worry that eventually the book she opened would be the last book. At this point all my words are borrowed, everything is in translation, about to be erased.

Retrato Imaginario

In the few days left before my untimely demise, I find myself making lists. My categories are simple: things I will have time to do and should do (burn certain papers) and things I will now never do (learn Catalan, make a soufflé, travel to Istanbul). The second list seems nearly endless; at some point it will have to list itself as one more unattainable desire, formed earlier by a consciousness which will soon cease to exist. The first list is quite short; after all I haven't lost my reason. Three days' time (less, actually) is hardly enough to do more than re-read Archilochos, *The Pleasures of C*, "Funes the Memorious," and a few choice pages of *Anna Karenina;* to eat ice cream (fortunately it's summer), walk about the neighborhood, and sort through the detritus of my life. And of course, sleep. If only I can sleep very well, and visit the theater of dreams a few more times. My sleep was a source of conflict throughout childhood; my parents were unable to understand my insomnia. Did they know how I would lie awake, counting to infinity, unable to float freely into dreams until the morning hours? Now I will never perfect the art of sleeping, for death is no sleep as far as I can tell. The dead I've encountered have lacked everything save a mysterious cellular activity of decay. No, my sleeping days will soon be over and the cities I visited in my dreams will pass to others, or die with me in a single exhalation. Also my ability to fly and my happy meetings with those long dead. Will I be asleep when it happens? The hour hasn't been predicted. Would I prefer to be at home or in the park? Would certain streets be preferable to others? I want to add some item to the list, such as "plan last day," but even as I write this, surrounded by children and people not much younger than myself, the hopelessness of such a task is overwhelming. My last day will surely be like any other. The world will continue, completely indifferent to me. I'm inclined to stay at home, so as not to trouble anyone. List 2: visit the sea one last time, travel through France by train, read Homer in Greek. The sun has sunk behind the roofs that form the western edge of the square. The cafés are filling up. Soon I'll ask for the check in the language I've started to learn. I'll pay my bill and start for home. The wind is cooler now. I'll open all the windows.

open book
for Edward

1.
The subject of all poems is the clock.

The subject of all poems is the skirt keeper rinsing and hanging her things out to dry.

The skirt keeper reminds me of little gowns, said S, whose story was just beginning outside the village.

Villagers are known for burning witches and burying adulteresses without their heads, you know. Be careful.

Careful with the little pitcher of milk. *Little pitchers,* my parents used to say around Christmastime, *have big...*

Big flowers clotted the hillside. A stone bigger than the flowers came tumbling down, gathering velocity as it came.

Cities don't feature in this story and they won't be mentioned again, nor hidden sneakily in other words.

In other words, they have pitchforks and anvils and stacks of hay and many of them are wearing aprons. Watch out!

S gathered her apron up and let it fall again, characteristically.

Character is revealed through small gestures, you know. She should smooth her apron rather than rumpling it in her tiny hands.

Not even the rain has such small hands.

Rain, rain, go away. Don't come back.

The backs of S's hands were quite nice and she knew it but pretended not to.

In some languages, pretend means *to try*.

There was a famous trial going on that S was dimly aware of. Well, maybe it wasn't famous yet, but it would be and that's what matters.

Household matters were *at sixes and sevens*. Some unlucky person would find herself on the street soon.

Do you get my meaning here?

Spoons and those special scissors meant for grapes, lustrous things, mostly from the kitchen.

Not much could be seen from the kitchen. A dooryard with chickens, which reminds me of another poem.

How white the gulls in gray weather.

But there were no gulls here nor gray weather since we told the rain to stop.

Stop right there! The suspense is killing me, interjected S, who'd felt she was being written about but hadn't known quite what to do about it.

About your story, I wrote, I have a mind to start erasing it…

DON'T!!!!!

Don't worry, you're safe for now, but can't you open your eyes and see that someone's stealing and there'll be trouble soon?

2.

S was clearly worried now and her work began to suffer. Also, she was beginning to find her pile of hay rather uncomfortable, so she asked the apothecary for a sleeping aid.

Sleep! You remember all the things Shakespeare had to say about it, don't you?

You're beginning to wonder who you are. I'm not surprised. Your mother predicted this one night when we were sitting up late drinking brandy and smoking.

Smoking is bad for your health. There are worse things, however.

She wondered how to liberate herself from certain obsessions that clouded her remarkably sunny disposition. Perhaps the apothecary, who had been so helpful before, could provide some wise suggestions.

To get wise is a phrasal verb meaning to learn something, usually about other people you thought trustworthy but now realize have been taking advantage of you in some way.

Cleaning, polishing, scrubbing, scouring, soaking, brushing, beating, rinsing, hanging, sweeping, mopping, dusting, wiping, sorting, folding.

She got wise to the fact that someone was disappearing shiny objects of value.

Meanwhile, a legal proceeding was carried out and more people were executed, along with some domestic animals who were shameless lawbreakers. Villagers were encouraged to bring their children to the spectacle, since it's never too early to instill morals in the people.

People always said she was a pretty girl.

A girl is the stuff myths are made on. Riding a fish, turning into a laurel tree, scattering breadcrumbs.

You had asked about the diet of serving girls during that period. I tried to assure you that gruel was the norm, but you were unconvinced. Offended, I withheld what I knew about beer poured over bread. Now you know all that I know.

Knowledge was confined to practical matters. What else could it be good for?

Can you get back to my story? S's voice had a shrill edge, although she was sleeping better.

Better to run while you can. The lady of the house has dark shadows under each eye and her fingertips are starting to fray.

I'm not afraid, squeaked S, *I haven't done anything!* And brushed a bit of straw from her hair.

You're wondering about the hairy man of the house. You expect him to be made of sausage and fur, with blood the color of a dog's lip.

Age begins to show around the lips.

One day she spilled a batch of ale across the kitchen flagstones. The old cook took this opportunity to divine future events. This led her to give S a beating she was unlikely to forget.

I noticed iris, ranunculus, anemones, primroses and forget-me-nots above us as we picnicked. And the ribbon of duck fat between the pâté and its crust. What did you notice?

What did I do? She kept repeating these four words and sobbing as she walked. The road out of town was black and soft with the moult of plane trees.

These trees are looking a bit parched. What do you say we turn the rain on again?

I'm not happy.

Happiness, it turns out, is more than a round loaf wrapped in white cloth, together with a block of sweet butter and your grandfather's pocket knife.

How do you say knife in this language? Neither of us could remember.

Remember where we started?

Startled birds rocketed up as she passed. Her boots were getting thinner. She was too afraid to sleep and too sore to sit.

A satisfied moon appeared in the sky.

Oh no, said S, *rain.*

3.
Should we have waited with the rain?

A wet girl found by the side of the road by hunters just before dawn.

Has it dawned on you yet where this is heading?

Phrasal verbs are quite difficult because they can't be linked to their meanings in a rational way. You must eat them whole, like oysters.

Oysters should be eaten only in certain places at certain times. This may not seem important now, but it's worth remembering.

I don't remember anything, sighed S to the little boy who woke her up in the field.

4.
It was the greatest day of his life so far. He had often found small skeletons and snakes and bits of interesting trash, but never a naked girl asleep in the clover.

How long have I been sleeping?

Her skin was almost blue, the color of whey. She found it difficult to move. Her rescuer tried to pull her up by a limp hand but tumbled back into thick green.

At some point the story will begin over again backwards. When that happens you'll know you've reached the middle.

Middle age, the middle ages.

Ages seemed to pass before he came back with his older sister. S would have spoken to the author during this time, but as I mentioned before, her memory was quite empty and clean.

The sister was a clean girl with a healthy fear of naked blue women. But her brother insisted, nearly jumping into the air.

Why are you belaboring this moment? someone said, and it was you in your bathrobe.

There's been a loss of consciousness, a number of notes played and erased. Actions omitted, left to the imagination.

The world is invented again for each person. Invented, invented, remembered, abandoned.

The little family wasn't happy to welcome an abandoned girl.

How can you call a family little that consists of a man, two wives, five children and unknown numbers of livestock and domestic animals?

Unknown to me. I'm sure he kept perfect count. Everyone in the village said he was very shrewd.

Before we go any further, let's stop for a cold drink.

I like a lot of ice with my drinks. With, rather than in. A separate glass of ice with a spoon.

The spoon thief from the other village was caught and punished. People were a bit disappointed in the stoic response of the thief to his punishment. Small children, especially, appeared bored; many were seen yawning atop their fathers' shoulders.

S woke up again in an unfamiliar pile of straw.

Can you remember anything?

But she didn't seem to hear the voice of her maker, which is quite common in the young.

Meanwhile, a heated conversation was going on in the bedroom of the man and his two wives, about the commonness of the foundling, the extra mouth to feed, etc., etc., etc.

As you used to say, the punishment for having more than one wife would be having more than one wife.

In another part of the house, a boy was asleep and dreaming of a field on fire, and all the field animals spilling out of it like grain and running every direction to get away.

The man of the house turned his back on one and looked at the other's back. Her hair was parted in a way he thought rather severe, which went with her personality. Even her private parts were starting to reflect a bitter outlook.

Look out! LOOK OUT!!! But S had fallen back asleep.

Young amnesiacs don't fall into your lap every day, he was thinking to himself.

That has to be an anachronism, you said from your chair by the window, and besides that a man like that wouldn't think in those words.

Who thinks in words anyway? Unless you're trying to learn a foreign language…

There's foreign and there are things that just don't make sense.

Sense and Sensibility is a very popular novel by Jane Austen, second only to *Pride and Prejudice* in terms of popularity. It concerns two daughters of a widowed mother and their struggles to marry well.

Well, he said, rolling over again to face the first one who always made him think of apples, *I think there's plenty of work for her to do here, and neither of you are getting any younger.*

What is this obsession with youth? You were pouring another cup of coffee. *It's getting a bit tedious!*

Coffee hadn't come to the land of our story at this time, nor had tea. Remember the beer over bread I mentioned earlier?

That would be for lunch. Before dawn one of the sisters of the family kicked at S with her tiny foot and pushed a bowl of porridge under her nose.

Fortunately she was able to grab up her bowl before a certain young and lively pig got his snout into it. There were pigs everywhere, a swarm of pink and brown and grey backs and legs and tails.

It had been the boy's job to deal with pigs, but now he found himself temporarily promoted to cows while his father sized up the work capacity of the new arrival. She might be quite simple after all, he mused, and not fit for much.

Much has been said about the restorative effects of the rural lifestyle and the romance of it, to the extent that people of means will actually pay to lodge themselves on family farms, and even send their children there to "work."

Children should be seen and not heard.

The children's day consisted of fourteen hours of work in the winter and sixteen in the summer, punctuated by sparse meals they would eat on the stone floor in the winter and outside in the chicken yard in the summer.

There was a little graveyard at the edge of the woods where some of their brothers and sisters slept and slept.

S was not popular with the children at first.

First you have to carry the slops out from the kitchen, said the boy, *being very careful not to spill anything because there isn't enough anyway.*

Enough is enough. We need to get S out of here before we die of boredom. Pigs! Slops! There are towns and villages and oceans out there!

There, warbled S, as she tipped the buckets over and watched the convergence of bristly backs.

She is a comely thing, the oldest brother was thinking, with her hair down her back like that and her face turning pink…

Meanwhile the wives were beginning to notice something everyone else was oblivious to: signs of pregnancy in our heroine.

5.
Heroines are few and far between.

Between the two wives, a plan was formed: to "lose" S on the way to or from the nearest village at fair time, which was just around the corner.

There really aren't any corners in the country. The "_____" perspective remains with us in expressions like this one. Obviously the author has spent some formative time in a place with bookshops, coffeehouses, taxicabs and professional cooks.

Time seemed to pass slowly in anticipation of the fair.
Everyone had a mountain of work to do, and the men were
scheduled to leave and return before the women, in order to
have the best chances with their livestock. At the last minute,
the plan hit a snag: the littlest boy (S's great defender)
contracted a fever and had to stay behind with the women.

Women. Apples. Mirrors. Poison. Breadcrumbs. Incantations.
Glass slippers. Stepmothers. He had never heard a story
before the one S told him the first night of the fever.

6.
The fever lasted for seven days.

Seven is an important number. Lucky seven, the seven seas,
etc.

It was lucky for S that she didn't go to the fair. Finally, she had
to stay home with the young Wil. She waved from the
doorway as the others departed in a crooked line.

Wil was in a state between sleep and waking. After the story
he had fallen into a dream that kept repeating. The funny
thing about it was the way real elements got confused and
woven in, like S's cool hand on his neck, or the bird that flew
into the room and flapped around madly until S caught it and
set it free.

It was on the fourth day of the fever that the madwoman
stopped by. She was also on her way to the fair but in dire
need of some clean water and a bit of bread.

Does it need to be said that S was unfamiliar with madwomen
but well-versed in tales of sorcery and divination?

My name is Klith, said the woman with her panpipe voice as she stood by the well. *There's a sick one about, isn't there?*

In S's view, Klith was an unusual woman. For starters, she was wearing a very thin shift with an ancient bodice of strange design. She carried a tapestry bag bulging with mysterious things, and a cup of fine metal on a slender chain around her neck. She had one brown eye which looked rather normal and an enormous blue eye.

Fix your eyes on this bag, said Klith.

S looked hard at the tapestry. Immediately she sensed something moving in the pattern. She saw a rabbit darting across the landscape, then other animals. She saw herself and Wil, running across fields, running and running.

Give the wee one a draught of this at sunset and sunrise, Klith's hand appeared from the bag with a little vial of purple liquor, *and mind your hearth, young miss!*

S sat down on the ground and watched Klith's progress up and down the nearby hills until she disappeared.

I know I saw something strange just now, thought S, and how did she know about Wil?

Wil had his first sip of madwoman's brew at sunset. He retched and coughed and wheezed in a way that made S question the potential efficacy of this remedy she had complete faith in.

Faith is a strange idea.

S's difficulties in sleeping began again. She was troubled by strange sensations and kept waking up with a start. Finally she collapsed into a deep slumber.

The fire started in the smallest hours when the moon was getting tired.

It was a small fire at first, just a few errant sparks blown out of the hearth by that wind that's supposed to drive people crazy.

In fact, it was the wind, and not the fire, that woke S up.

Wake up, she screamed, as she ran to Wil's bed.

If you fix your eyes on the page, you can see a girl streaming fire and carrying a little boy as she runs.

7.
This page will be different from the others.

Others may not understand what is happening.

Happiness is a ________________.

________________ means something to fill in yourself.

The self is always going from one thing to the next.

Next thing you know some time has passed.

Past tenses are useful for filling in the blanks.

Blink!

Blink again!

Against all odds.

Odd how things seem to go *from bad to worse.*

The worst would be stopping.

That would definitely be the worst.

That simply wouldn't do.

Do what?

What?

DO WHAT?

Oh it's YOU!

Of course, chimed S.

7.
Lucky seven, remember?

S remembered everything.

Well, not quite EVERYthing, thank goodness.

It was good to lie in the long wet grass and look up at the stars.

Wil was mending the burnt dress by tying former pieces of his nightshirt here and there in a very careful way that is not easy to describe.

Parts of S were unmendable. But slaked by night grass almost forgettable.

Wil regarded S's whiteness.

Snow White, fluted S lazily, *Rose Red.*

Rosy-fingered dawn was just around the corner.

8.

A wheel of starlings woke them up from their nap.

Naps are quite useful, all year round.

Wil was happy. He'd always wanted to run away from home and sleep outside with someone better than his mothers.

Mothers are hard to keep out of stories. They wait until you aren't looking, then come in and tidy things up or point out mistakes or ask why they haven't been mentioned and whether you had a happy childhood.

Little Red Riding Hood, yawned S, *do you know that one?*

Wil knew they'd better start walking.

Walking, over *hill and dale* pregnant, half-burned and half-dressed, isn't every character's dream come true.

The truth is that S really had no other choice. At least she remembered she was being written. Maybe that would help her at some point, although *IT SURE HASN'T HELPED YET* she thought in capital letters.

OH! You can read what I'm thinking!

Of course. I just didn't want to embarrass you before.

Hmph.

Walking, walking,

walking, walking, walking, walking, walking, walking, walking,
walking, walking, walking, walking, walking, walking, walking,
walking, walking, walking, walking, walking, walking, walking,
walking, walking, walking, walking, walking, walking, walking,
walking, walking, walking, walking, walking, walking, walking,
walking, walking, walking, walking, walking, walking..........

9.

… and waking in fields of rye and under giant oaks and next
to rings of ancient stones and other prepositions with other
features in a landscape less and less familiar to them.

The family's homecoming is none of our business and in fact
we know nothing about it.

Who's "we"?

The correct placement of the quotation marks with regard to
punctuation is mysterious to me. British and American usage
differs.

As S was confused by handedness, being naturally left-handed
but made to use her right hand after a wise woman (mad
woman?) warned her mother she might become a criminal if
allowed to continue in her southpawism.

Criminal, as in arsonist, kidnapper, thief, etc.

They trudged along. Wil was on the lookout for small animals
he might hang in the noose he'd made from a long stalk. He
hadn't been successful with this yet, but remained convinced
that his method would work on the right unsuspecting
creature.

S wasn't feeling very well but didn't suspect the true nature of her condition.

When Ahmed saw them on the road his first instinct was to hide, and this is worth remembering.

Remember that story about Ali Baba and the forty thieves? inquired Wil out of the side of his mouth.

S elbowed him in the side.

Good morning, mistress and young master! His voice seemed to echo off the clouds. *Well met!*

10.

Ahmed had met many travelers but he admitted in his night devotion that these two struck him as unusual. He was very polite, even in his thoughts. So polite, in fact, that the reader will be spared a transcription, which would be lengthy and full of thanks and grace.

He found the girl awkward yet graceful and the boy clever, strong and honest. The girl might be with child. Their clothes were half unraveled and they gave vague answers about their village and their people. Parts of the girl appeared to be bandaged and the boy had a bad cough.

He asked his god what to do and waited for an answer. In the meantime he changed his course to accompany them a ways and safeguard them until they reached a decent village.

11.

1. Will a "decent village" appear, and if it does, will it welcome a black man traveling with a pregnant serving girl and a little peasant boy?

2. What country are we in?

3. Where was Ahmed going?

4. Is the family looking for Wil?

5. What will happen when S realizes she's pregnant?

6. What is the British vs. American rule for the placement of
the quotation mark?

7. What are they finding to eat?

8. Why do they call left-handers southpaws?

12.
Let's pause a minute by the side of the book. In this country,
it's summertime.

Time for stone fruit and fireworks.

Works of semi-precious stone inlaid in gold and silver.

You're reading a book about gold, slaves, ships and crosses.

Crossing the room with a towel.

Another day subsides, settles into embers.

I was never embarrassed as a child. My world was wholly
imaginary.

13.
They were stopped in the road by a line of men carrying a
holy relic in an ornate wooden shrine mounted on two long
poles.

A relic is a piece of a saint, isn't it?

Wil noted that some of the men looked like skeletons. He had a story to tell about a skeleton but thought it might be best to save it for another time.

Time was unable to pass around the relic parade. It stopped and rested a moment, invisible under an oak tree.

Lined with oaks, this was a popular road. It led to the land of Woden in one direction. Where did the other one go?

Our merry band was going the Woden way.

With his brothers, Woden fashioned the earth and the sky from the dead body of the giant Ymir, and from an ash tree and an alder he created the first man and woman.

S was the first woman Ahmed had ever taken a long walk with. He usually walked ahead, so as not to seem to be staring at her from behind.

Her behind was rather nice. He had noticed this but kept it out of his thought language, which was the thought that really counted anyway.

Anyway, S went on, *then we ran away as fast as we could.* This was the last sentence of an incredibly long and detailed account of S's entire life and Wil's entire life as much as she knew it.

Wil had listened closely to the tale, just in case there was any new information to be gained. He had decided during the night that S was the woman of his life and now had the new pain of desperate jealousy lest she should betray an interest in any other male past or present.

Presently, a town will come into to view, praise Allah!

Town might be a bit of an exaggeration.

Two churches, a number of public houses, a gallows, a small prison, a market and a cluster of dwellings all made from the same stone. And a noisy bunch of washing girls slapping wet garments and singing.

The singing stopped at the sight of Ahmed.

This is a bad sign, he thought politely.

Twelve eyes watched our trio enter town. No doubt there were many more gazing out of slits in the stone, but those unseen will remain uncounted.

14.
Meanwhile, back at the burnt farmhouse, things were going rather badly. The man of the house was beside himself and let the skins of all present remember this fact. Bruised, bloody, tired, stiff, footsore and without very much shelter left them, the family slept outside in beds of hay.

He lay staring up at the sky, thinking of certain curves S had that he was particularly interested in. *Fuck these goddamned fucking bright stars!* He shouted, and turned over to sleep.

In the morning a party of vigilantes set out to retrieve the arsonist/kidnapper and bring her to justice.

15.
Wil realized before anyone else that a festival was getting underway in the village. A fan of festivals, he turned to say something to

S, who had turned her head to hear something that Ahmed
was saying softly

into her other ear.

It was at just this moment that a good-sized pony cart
careened into the path and knocked Wil to the ground before
covering him with a good amount of dirt and nearly
squashing him under hoof and wheel.

Ahmed noticed that the driver neither slowed nor turned back
to look at his work.

Ahmed gathered Wil up in his arms.

Ahmed did a bit of engraving in his quiet mind: a cart with
two fat ponies, loaded with rough timber and driven by

a someone.

S was hopping about like a bird.

The afore-mentioned uncounted eyes watched everything.

16.
There are lots of injuries in this work, as you've probably
noticed by now. We are taking part in a world of scalds and
bruises and rough men and women who haven't much truck
with table manners and *please* and *thank you* and conversations
in the drawing room. However, any competent librarian can
recommend another work which contains ladies with white
hands and young people who want to improve their situations
through marriage and the comings and goings of people of
leisure, in which fabrics and spring mornings are lovingly
described.

17.
It's impossible to describe what happened next.

18.
You had just returned from a brief trip to a hot country. *That's not fair,* you said. A ring of water had formed around the base of your drink and I went to get a napkin. *You have to say what happened next.*

All at once, the village came into the streets, as if cued by an invisible hand.

Wil was torn out of Ahmed's arms and carried away by men in skins with wicker masks.

Ahmed himself was taken into custody by the town officials, whose masks were made of cloth.

S was dragged to the church and made to pray on her white knees against the cold round stones. She didn't understand the language being spoken, or what she was supposed to be praying for.

Four days passed and S spent them scrubbing and performing other gerunds having to do with keeping a church fit for the eyes of ____, which see everywhere, even around the tiniest corner.

Wil spent them praying to be released from the stable in which he was chained up and fed very strange things by masked men who sang songs he couldn't understand.

I can't say how Ahmed spent this time. His modesty, his beautiful shame, forbids it.

19.
Days in a hot country. You spent them on a small balcony and in the half-shaded streets. Experience is incommunicable.

The ability to predict the future would come in handy here, thought Ahmed (this is a rough translation, of course). Things look rather bad.

He had suffered, but his suffering was diluted by his concern for the others. He reflected that their odd combination of fragility and relentlessness was what had attracted him to them in the first place.

Many places now have plaques commemorating this and that which you can linger in front of on foot after you've stopped for lunch and consulted the guide book.

This particular place had seen a good deal of arguing over the centuries about whether tourists would be attracted or repelled by the historical goings-on there. *Of course it depends on your taste, people would say, and on fashion. During the time of the guillotine we were very popular.*

17.
Where were we?

Who's "we," anyway?

What would you do, if you were me?

Are you talking to me? you said from the kitchen.

Are you talking to me? whispered S from page 41.

*No, I'm talking to you, the one reading this, you there, who just
turned the page. What would you do?*

18.
Everyone is waiting for your answer.

19.
While we're all waiting, the small band of vigilantes has made
some progress in their search for the young
arsonist/kidnapper known as S. Remember them? A group of
rough and smelly peasants armed to the teeth with sharp
objects and looking for a good time along the way.

Which way did they go? This way and that, according to the
wisdom of S's former employer, their erstwhile leader in all
things vigilante. They had reached the Village of C., about a
two days walk from the village in which their prey was
scouring the church surfaces under the glare of various thick
matrons and pale clergy.

We'll find that little bitch! shouted Wil's dad for the umpteenth
time, as he drained his horn-handled cup. For once no one
shouted in assent. The others, as much as they were enjoying
this romp about the countryside, were beginning to wonder
what the women back home were getting up to, and how
much longer they could live on the few worn coins they
fingered as they drank.

Uh hum, one cleared his throat delicately. *Mmmm xxxxmmm,*
added another. They were drinking slowly and looking into
their cups between drinks. A third started to snore, a fourth
stepped from the shabby little dining room into the yard to
find a secluded tree.

WhadoIcareboutthagirlanyway? he asked the tree as he watered it. *Whasitome?*

This was a rather young tree, the son of a much older one that had, until quite recently, stood nearby. It had been a sad day, the day of his father's death. The remains were piled against the little building the man had come out of; the scent of his father billowed out of the chimney. Maybe that was the worst of it. You really couldn't avoid it.

Have you read Georges Perec's book *A VOID*? It's the one without the letter E. I confess I haven't read it. Actually, I haven't read much of Perec's work.

Wil's dad was about to pass out. See? No E's. But this was just an accident. I bet if you did it on purpose it would be much harder.

For one thing, no E's would mean no trees, unless you called them by name. Then you could have oak, ash, and birch at least. But a lot of them would be left out, like the wet one, who happened to be an elder.

Wil's dad put his head down on the table. The others took this opportunity to have a brief conference in the yard before they made their quiet exeunt through the back fence. The young elder heard everything.

20.
Ahmed was having a long dream which seemed to take place under water. The water was unbearably beautiful, like being inside a jewel. His mother was holding him while a thousand tiny fish brushed against them caressingly.

Wil was unable to sleep. He had lost his trust of the night. Strange things might happen to him if he closed his eyes. He might never wake up. Or wake to something horrible that had started while he was asleep.

S was pretending to be blind. As she found herself in total darkness, this wasn't that difficult, but it seemed to help. She'd pretended this sometimes as a little girl, to see if she could make her way around the room without looking. Could she find her skirt and shoes? Now she braided the cleaning rags she'd been hiding in her sleeves.

Sleep! That knits up the raveled sleave of care!

Shhhhhhhh! Hissed little s, *don't wake anyone!*

Anyone who isn't completely frustrated by this story by now is your voice was overwhelmed by a motorbike and I didn't ask you to repeat yourself but nodded in a way that might suggest a variety of things. We were walking down a street in ___________. I promised earlier that there would be no ___________ in this narrative, not even masked ones.

The masked men of the village were having problems sleeping. This should give you some idea of how exciting their plans were. Meanwhile the festival rolled along, with its particular daily rituals.

Rituals are culturally specific. Ahmed was trying to remember this. He was trying to send telepathic messages of hope to his friends.

S had no friends in the village, but she did have a fetus in her belly. One of the church women noticed this and asked ___ for some instructions on how to proceed.

I mean, it's obvious that some unrealistic rescue is going to take place, some magical workaround. You signaled the waiter for the check.

Some signal from ____. What would it be? The church woman didn't know. She imagined, though, that it would be something really out of the ordinary.

Ordinarily I wouldn't say anything, but I think it's important to be honest.

After all, it wouldn't be right to kill an honest future mother if ____ disapproved, would it?

Ahmed's telepathic messaging was a complete failure. The future had stopped for S and for Wil.

Of course, the future doesn't really exist, thought Ahmed. *I don't blame them for being caught up in the moment.* He could feel the stones under S's knees, and felt for the first time that she was expecting a child. He started to cry. Wil must be just asleep, he thought. He hasn't started dreaming yet.

In fact, Wil had just fallen asleep, much against his volition. Now his task was to keep the theater of dreams as dark as possible.

The theater is a place of many superstitions. Like the one about whistling. You're not supposed to. Do you know why?

Why is a question we mustn't ask very much.

Excuse me?

You heard what I said.

Who's speaking, please?

Never mind.

No, I'm serious. I want you to identify yourself.

Why don't you identify YOURself?

I'm the author. Who are you?

Hello?

21.
Who are you trying to fool with this? A few toast crumbs were
stuck to your fingers. *I think you should take a little break and
write something else, or at least READ something. The whole thing,*
a bite of toast, a sip of tea, *is getting very morbid and sadistic
anyway. And I don't believe,* another sip, *you take it very seriously.
I mean as a piece of writing. Clearly it has some strange appeal to
you emotionally.* Swallow, glance into cup, napkin to lips. *To be
honest, I'm a little worried about you. Are you getting enough sleep?*

Sleep keeps coming up. You could say it's a theme, the way
we used talk about themes in books when I was a girl
growing up. The most common themes, as far as I remember,
were "loss of innocence" or "coming of age."

Age, middle age, the middle ages.

Ages ago, S was a girl cleaning spoons in a little house near
the village of X. Now she's about to be a mother, if we can
get her out of the predicament she's in.

*In terms of things you might read, let me know if you'd like a
recommendation.*

Reading was not recommended for women at various
moments in history. It was perceived as leading them into
immoral ways: perhaps it would be more accurate to say that
reading created desires.

I began my sexual life as a "desiring subject." It was only later on that I became concerned with being a "desired object."

That's not true.

Shut up. What do you know about it?

You're lying! Why are you lying?

22.
S was lying on the ground behind the church. She wasn't sleeping, but rather *resting her eyes.* She was tied to the church door by a rope around her waist, which sounds inefficient but in fact it worked very well to keep her from running away.

We used to sing "Away in a Manger" at Christmastime. I can tell you now that it was probably my least favorite.

At least she could stretch out her not-very-long legs and point her very tired toes.

This can't go on very much longer, S was thinking. *I'm soooooooooo tired.*

Red was not a popular color in the time of S, Wil and Ahmed. It was an expensive dye, and not worn much by ordinary people. I don't believe, however, that it had the sexual significance made so famous by Nathaniel Hawthorne later on.

Later on everything will become clear, mused Ahmed. He believed in a divine pattern.

Soon, we'll hear the *pitter-patter of little feet.*

Or the big galumphing steps of…

Wil's father.

He hadn't forgotten her small inviting frame. He had actually forgotten Wil, whom he'd never paid much attention to and couldn't have picked out of a lineup.

Waking up after the departure of his neighbors and former friends, he found himself in a foul mood. His weather went unimproved by the discovery that his pockets were empty. Fortunately everyone was out at that moment, spending a bit of windfall. Otherwise there would have been hell to pay.

Asked "where jazz was going," Thelonious Monk replied, *it can go to hell for all I care.*

Remember the *raveled sleave?*

Wil's dad's was rather unknit.

He decided to head for home.

A severe migraine impaired his sense of direction, however, and he was soon entering the village by a pretty little road that led past the rear churchyard, where our heroine was resting her eyes.

I don't believe it, you said, crossing the living room with a newspaper.

The newspaper comes with a little gift on the weekends. Currently this gift is one in a series of books in English and the official language of this country, on facing pages. These small books are generally very, very bad. We have all of them together on the bookshelf.

Ahmed's books had been taken from his pack and torn into

about nine million pieces preparatory to burning them as part of the festivities that were keeping the men of the village full of adrenaline and high spirits.

These included the works of Homer and Archilochos along with a holy book and an herbal which Ahmed had been writing for five years.

It seems like years, thought Ahmed, *since I've seen the sea.*

Was Ahmed's sea the same as Homer's sea? He felt that it was. He'd seen it wine-dark, silver as the sky, torn in white shreds.

He endeavored to clear his mind, to smooth it with his sea memory.

Happiness, said Ingrid Bergman, *is good health and a bad memory.*

Wil's father was neither short nor tall, stout nor lean. He wasn't a man you'd remember if you saw him at the laundromat, or in an elevator.

He saw some laundresses beating clothes with paddles against a stone trough.

Good ladies, he intoned, *would you be so kind as to tell me the name of this town?*

It's good to add a bit of salt to sweet things. A pinch, a sprinkle.

A headache, empty pockets and a six hour walk hadn't taken the twinkle out of Wil's father's eye.

I think I've forgotten to mention that Wil had lost consciousness at this point.

Torture concerns itself with both remembering and forgetting.

Why are you torturing them? You were reading over my
shoulder.

As he walked on, the laundresses commented on his broad
shoulders and strong-looking ass.

Do you ever ask this question?

This is a moment of suspension. Smoke hangs in the air,
making light more visible.

Sometimes it's helpful to blend into the landscape.

Landscape painting had yet to be invented. The one painter at
work in the village was busy gilding the book in a saint's
hands. Although he had rarely seen a book, he remembered
that the edges of the pages could be gold, and that a thin
leather ribbon could tie the covers closed.

The lovers had smoke, champagne and kisses.

But that was in another country, and besides…

It takes time to understand the culture of your country.
Sometimes you must leave it to begin to see its strange ways
for what they are.

23.
We need to find a way out of this.

24.
This and that. These and those.

These are really country people. It's important to take that
into account.

The village was in the ancient region of Ours. It was called St. Eustache-en-Ours, and was officially ruled over by the Comte d'Ours. He was a quiet, studious man who liked to spend his afternoons reading beside a window twice his height. His residence was distinguished by its blue spires and rooftops that were several shades darker than the summer sky.

Our little band of detainees will not be saved be the Comte, nor by Wil's dad, asleep by the wall of Le Petit Ours, which was a fine little inn by any standard.

No, they'll be saved by the painter.

Paintings are made of many things. He was experimenting with egg white and gold dust when the festival began.

Fucking peasants, he muttered. (This is a rough translation of the regional Oursian dialect.)

Painters are known to be irascible, especially when they're running out of eggs.

Most of the village men were running through the streets in white robes with red hoods that covered their faces and culminated in points above their heads. Meanwhile, the children and their mothers and grandmothers made a deafening clamor by drumming on all manner of skin, wooden and metal objects.

The priests of the village came behind the runners and drummers. They were accompanied by a strange group of dancers dressed in black and adorned with human bones.

Then the ox cart with Ahmed, Wil and a number of pigs and goats.

Then S, on a small white pony led by two men in white surplices.

Finally there came a ragged band of monks with St. Eustache-en-Ours' great treasure: half of the saint's ear in a beautiful antique reliquary.

The painter's name was Antoine. He had a family name, but his acquaintances in the village (he had no friends there) always called him Monsieur Antoine. An unmarried man no longer young but by no means old, he was perennially subject to advances by families with marriageable girls. His relentless rejection of these offers led to extensive speculation about his sexual habits.

Just at the moment, however, his mind was full of eggs, or rather the need for eggs.

Eggs have restorative powers. If you should lose your appetite, eggs are recommended. Soft boiled, or poached, with a slice or two of good toast.

The village executioner was slitting the throat of the first pig. A great roar went up through the crowd.

Have I mentioned that St. Eustache-en-Ours was famous for its crows?

A huge flock of them lived in the towering plane trees surrounding the village. Grandmothers threatened the little ones with tales of abduction by those enormous black birds.

Grandmothers, wolves, baskets and cloaks; match-sellers, mermaids, magic beans.

S was enclosed in a strange basket-like contraption when Antoine spotted her on the wooden dais decorated with leaves. It looked like a birdcage made of bent willow branches.

Who's the brains of this outfit? he wondered.

In high school physiology, we dissected sheep's brains. Pickled in formaldehyde, they yielded to the blade with a slight crunch.

Actually, Antoine didn't think in those words at all.

His flash of recognition and horror was wordless.

There were no less than a few thousand people filling the Place de St. Eustache. This should help to illustrate the importance of this feast day to the region of Ours.

Speaking of feast, the women had been cooking and baking for days. Among dishes of wild boar with prunes, pâté en croute and the region's famous sausages and cheeses, the spicy scent of "delice d'Ours" wafted through the narrow streets.

Forgive me for making St. Eustache sound better than it was. I have a weakness for good cooking.

Looking at S, as best he could through the crowd, Antoine struggled to think clearly. A man next to him slapped him on he back and said something unintelligible.

A number of pigs and goats had been slaughtered by now and the executioner had stopped his work to drink out of a wooden cup. Meanwhile, his assistant took this opportunity to sharpen a large two-headed axe and demonstrate its edges on a few chicken feathers.

Ahmed continued the prayer he'd been repeating for the past sixteen hours. He no longer bothered to say it only in his head, but let the syllables flow into the midday air.

The Olympian gods could be felt on the Trojan plain: as a radiance, a change of light and air.

Antoine was chiefly a painter of angels. This may come as a surprise to those who have seen his work. He's really known for saints. Saints were his business, his bread and butter, but angels were his specialty, the love of his life, his vocation.

25.
Sing, O muse...

Ahmed's prayer was getting mixed up now with his other readings. The image of a white sail came to comfort him. He tried to send it on to Wil, to S.

S had been hoisted up in her cage for all to see.

S is for sound, symbol, saraband, sycamore, syllogism, summer.

Years later, when he reflected on this moment, M. Antoine would remember it as devoid of sound—utterly silent. He would see himself as flying through the crowd, his mouth a tunnel of black with red behind it.

STOOOOOOOOOOOOOOOOOOOOOOOOOOOOOOOOOOOOOO OOOOOOOOOOOOOOOOOOOOOOOOOOOOOOOOOOOOOO OOOOOOOOOOOOOOOOOOOOOOOOOOOOOOOOOOOOOO OOOOOOOOOOOOOOOOOOOOOOOOOOOOOOOOOP!!!!!!!!!! !!

This is, of course, a translation. What's important here is the overall effect. Those interested in reading more about this episode should refer to R. Amiens' little-known but worthwhile volume: *Les Anges de St. Eustache-en-Ours.*

Our weather is clearly changing. But who can say what the future holds?

The executioner and his assistant kept hold of S. They were, after all, professionals.

Everyone started shouting. The curate had to come forward on the dais and quiet things down. No one could hear what he said to Antoine. Crows wheeled around the square.

The curate's jaw was very prominent, as though cut from rose-colored stone. In fact, this very jaw can be seen in a number of Antoine's works. Although he badgered him for years, the curate would never sit for a proper portrait; he preferred to lend his features to saints and the occasional Roman soldier.

Antoine stepped forward and faced the crowd.

This woman, he shouted, *is my daughter.*

It was so quiet you could hear a baby snoring in her mother's womb.

Perhaps that's an exaggeration. But it was very, very quiet.

Ahmed's white sail rippled, flapped, then caught the wind and billowed out, round as a cello.

native speaker
for the clouds

Dear ___________,

People are small here. But you know that already, I imagine.
Un-small, I walk until my feet are sore, until I feel the bones.
Yours in thin socks and good shoes; you have a sense of
quality. I suppose your family was aristocratic, they must have
been, yet you spread your arms wide. You laugh, you use
idiomatic expressions. A character in a novel would return to
you as mirror, as memory. You wouldn't hesitate. *God is in the
details,* in a broken fingernail. Almond body, clothed in its
own sense of itself.

Dear _________,

Thank you for your absence, your useful disappearance, air's
cave where your form imprints late August light. Wanted in
sand, in thick sheets. Your mother watches television. Her
hands retired. Your brother scrubs in and makes a first
incision. A country is clothing, the cut of a jacket. Price of
cologne, nuance of speech. Words, tiny as salt. What did you
want to be? Instructions on a box, a game of cards. The men
are playing now, in your harbor.

Dear _________,

October already and time is flowing, flooding, leaking out of
our windows and walls. I wander the shops, hungry, empty of
ideas. Sleeping is my best work. You are driving, listening to
music, without appetite. Here it's time for lamplight,
something bitter on the tongue.

Dear _________,

Aren't we supposed to be old enough for this, or too old? And what is the point of this spiraling, if nothing is to be discovered? You wore linen in the hot months. But that's a different story. I was thinking of age and predictability and logistics of course. I miss your accent and your eyes. Your slender fingers and your stories. Maybe I'm not old enough yet, wrapped up like a baby, shedding silver strands. Glasses, lamplight, what this table remembers. *Salad days.* A wheel of remembered light.

Dear _________,

Coordinates. Where a crime might take place or be imagined, where you had a certain dream.

Dear _________,

Failure to settle. Giant egg breaks, vestige of ourselves previously as others. He dragged his broom like a tail, she had so much energy. Teaching language, what's possible, what's desirable, what doesn't fit. Social agreements, a gray evening full of dog. Who is thinking of you? You are a lamp, a pair of gloves. Our bells are made of lesser metals lacking richness. Time falls, is blown down the street, made dirty as it goes.

Dear ________,

Tea with sugar. A red coat, wet fur. The earnestness of things, their qualities given, offered. How to care for the self, for anything, difficult. Tea at dusk. Embrace of a sweater, what belonged to someone else, someone you weren't sure you loved, but loved, anyway. A boy, a boy's room.

Dear _________,

Against remembering. A series of sums, easy enough. You must count the trees before you sell the forest. Birds, vines, a river, unexpectedly cold. Don't be disappointed, keep adding and subtracting. How your jacket fits, the price of being unhappy. But those weren't your words. You said, *for the same price you could have been happy.*

Dear _________,

I continue unprepared, frustrated, the wrong side of something. The soles of my feet are hot, I have a runny nose. Why don't I dye my hair, turning whiter by the day? An ache swelters and spreads. Her hands were wet and it slipped from them and smashed. No remedy for this.

Dear _________,

Extremities likely to become numb, *to fall asleep.* You are also a writer, a storyteller, a maker of event. Figs, milk, butter, couscous. Tongue slightly burnt. Money flying, falling, swirling at your feet. If you could only come with me everywhere as my chooser, my discerner. *If there's no problem,* she told us, *a guy will come on Friday.* How did you learn the language—did you learn it in bed?

Dear __________,

One continuous mistake. Where is the pleasure in that? Or is this beside the point? I fell gracefully, without sound. I mean to say: the air was stirred.

Dear __________,

Mid-November already and rain. Snowflakes on the part of
the map which designates mountains. A martini, the dream of
glass and near darkness. You in every season, a horizon line of
sand and shining leaves. You know how to wait and what to
do, how to make ways. Do you really think nothing is hidden?

Dear __________,

Thinner than thin. And mine behind a closed door. Where am
I when the action takes place? With you, perhaps, over a late
lunch. Try again. Ask for something else this time.

Dear __________,

Mysteries of language. Your mistakes are sweet, of course.
Part of what I love of you. I overestimate. The wrong shoes
and no socks, a cold day of wind blowing clouds towards the
sea. You are working and working and—what is your
consolation? Consolation for what?

Dear __________,

How I miss you! Clouds uncertain of their direction, a long
night ahead. Vendors of butane. November. We didn't worry
about the price of light and you called your girls *baby*. I'm a
foreigner now, like you.

Dear __________,

Alive inside a painting. Northern light. Blue kimono, one side
over the other. There is a correct way to do each thing. We
have our rituals, and what we've learned in the dark. You are
secretive, good at hiding things.

Dear __________,

You are sleeping. Lights strung all over town, more than ever.
Coffee with milk. Catalan. The times you drove before dawn.
Your country: hidden, remembered. What you hoped for or
expected, which never came, a part of your past.

Dear _________,

The Nat King Cole school of Spanish. I fear that I'm not communicating well and it's been a long time since I've spoken this language, if I've ever spoken it at all. He would stand by my table and look at me. He would make intricate and time-consuming gifts. Change of state, change of address. I'm *not from around here.*

Dear _________,

He made tea for me with a portable gas burner, the kind
you'd take camping. Not you, of course, you would never do
that, I mean *one*. The formality drifting out of our language,
the one you speak so well. I mean you particularly. The
Chinese lantern shifts slightly from the rising heat. Two
bookish sorts bundled up in sweaters, coats and scarves,
sharing this beloved table.

Dear _________,

The end of the beginning. But this is also untrue, or a half truth, a way of narrating something. A limit in the lungs, outrider of a week in bed. *Dead iambics.* Sometimes I want to throw my ash spear into the street. Where is that warm stone edge I've dreamt of for so long?

Dear _________,

Indelible images I borrow when I fail to make my own. Young tree, old woman. Naked under kimono. How to fold, which over which. Slender as a birch. There are paper houses in Japan. Crowds, trains, cups of tea. No way to speak.

Dear _________,

Cold seeps through the floor. Trucks are being loaded and unloaded; we've entered the season of things. Lights, chocolates, watches: a great market is being opened. Tired, breathless. Quick bird heart. Each day a tiny door opens.

Dear _________,

Heat and light. Hammering. That north African language you
hear in the narrow streets. The year is about to turn, to
become a series of notes.

Dear _________,

Cowboys. Bankrobbers, trainrobbers, diamond thieves. Such-
and-such street, where I was sitting on a bench, years ago, a
day the color of ashes. The notes you play, the notes you
don't play.

Dear _________,

You are asleep, but are you dreaming?

Dear __________,

Old year, old night, time's stain unmoved by this rinsing. A set of instructions: how to encounter one completely new or dreamt of or hoped for, one unexpected, marked by time, by contradictions. *Forest of paradox.* And there at the edge of a clearing, one poplar, barely leafed.

Dear __________,

Sixth day of winter. Cold, rain. An architect's writing. The measure of concertos, their silences. Framework of stringed instruments: these ribs were there then, or some version of them, milk inside the fig-dark flesh. Time, light, form, measure, patience.

Dear __________,

Mid-winter spring. You are turning in your sleep. Do you remember your dreams? A man will hide, will close doors. Bluest possible and warm, a day to wish on. Tea and couscous, cinnamon, hours, minutes, and your ritual of dressing and undressing. I console myself with __________. And you?

Dear _________,

My temporal education is beginning now, in branches beyond wrought iron. I knew something about minutes but nothing about years. A pale day without shadows. Building façades waver in the glass. Will repetition finally teach me the things I don't want to learn?

Dear __________,

Postures of waiting and wet under the arms. How many
women? You scent yourself, you think about the prices of
things. I remember music in your voice and certain words you
delighted in. Footsteps, the creak of a door, white breath of
the heater. The way you would greet a dog. Your summer
clothes.

Dear __________,

Will I complete myself here? In city streets or olive leaves?
Light curves around the planet. Windows of buildings trade
ingots through the hours.

Dear __________,

Hot coffee with milk. Hazy light. A few Cole Porter songs and
the pleasure of rhyming. Doormen, little shops, the old ways
of doing things, a sense of value. What to repair, what to
throw away. A season turning to slag, to new leaves. What did
you want? What were you planning?

Dear ________,

Cello suite #1. Memories of certain walls, pictures in a
museum, *where yellow leaves or none.* You would like this
country. Certainly I'm making mistakes. Small ones, chained
and disordered, and one long one, the one of my life. But
lamplight will console you, and girls in boots, and finding
someone you've been waiting for—

Notes

Valerie Coulton is the author of *The Cellar Dreamer* (Apogee Press), *passing world pictures* (Apogee Press), and *The Lily Book* (San Francisco State University). Her work has appeared in *Front Porch, kadar koli, New American Writing, Parthenon West Review,* and *e-poema,* among other periodicals. She lives in Barcelona with the poet Edward Smallfield.

OTHER POETRY TITLES FROM APOGEE PRESS

Maxine Chernoff
Among the Names
The Turning

Valerie Coulton
The Cellar Dreamer
open book
passing world pictures

Tsering Wangmo Dhompa
In the Absent Everyday
My rice tastes like the lake
Rules of the House

Kathleen Fraser
Discrete Categories Forced into
Coupling

Paul Hoover
Edge and Fold

Alice Jones
Gorgeous Mourning

Stefanie Marlis
cloudlife
fine

Edward Kleinschmidt Mayes
Speed of Life

Pattie McCarthy
bk of (h)rs
Table Alphabetical of Hard Words
Verso

Denise Newman
Human Forest
Wild Goods

Elizabeth Robinson
Also Known As
Apostrophe
Apprehend

Edward Smallfield
equinox
The Pleasures of C

Cole Swensen
Oh

Truong Tran
dust and conscience
four letter words
placing the accents
within the margin

TO ORDER OR FOR MORE INFORMATION GO TO WWW.APOGEEPRESS.COM